BEING WEIRD

EMBRACING WEIRDNESS

KEVIN B DIBACCO

MULTIMEDIA

Copyright © 2024 by Kevin B. DiBacco
All rights reserved.

CONTENTS

KEVIN'S REMARKABLE JOURNEY OF STRENGTH, RESILIENCE AND WEIRDNESS!

Kevin's lifelong passion for powerlifting and fitness has been nothing short of remarkable. His journey has been marked by numerous challenges, both physical and mental, yet he has persevered with unwavering determination. Kevin's path took an unexpected turn when he faced a three-year recovery from back surgery, coupled with the daunting prospect of not returning to his work at the Production Studio.

During this challenging period, Kevin experienced firsthand the depths of depression. His journey into darkness was met with courage and a commitment to healing. For two years, he worked tirelessly with counselors, psychotherapists, and mental health professionals to overcome this formidable obstacle. This experience gave Kevin invaluable insight into the nature of depression and the path to recovery.

Today, while Kevin still occasionally grapples with feeling down, he has developed robust coping mechanisms and a deep understanding of mental health. His book, "Depression: Understanding and Overcoming," is written from the perspective of someone who has truly been there, offering authentic and compassionate guidance to others facing similar struggles.

Kevin's medical history reads like an orthopedic textbook, a testament to both his military service and his lifelong dedication to fitness. As a proud veteran who served in the USAF security forces, Kevin is officially recognized as a service-connected disabled veteran. His list of injuries and surgeries is extensive: 6 knee operations, 2 major back surgeries, 2 hip replacements, brain surgery, and brain radiation. Some of these injuries stem from his time in service, while others are the result of his intense dedication to powerlifting and his active lifestyle. But no amount of adversity could extinguish his inner fire and drive.

At the age of 62, Kevin undertook a monumental fitness journey to shed 60 pounds (ca. 27 kg), proving that age is just a number. His passion for health and fitness remained undimmed by the passing years. Through all the ups and downs, Kevin persevered with an indomitable spirit.

He now aims to share his hard-won wisdom with others who are facing adversity. Drawing from his experiences in the military, his personal health battles, and his career challenges, Kevin developed "ISO QUICK STRENGTH," a program designed to help people rebound after setbacks. He recognized that overcoming difficulties requires both physical and mental strength.

Kevin spreads his message of resilience and determination through a blog, books, and his personal mantra: "Those who quit will always fail." These simple yet powerful words encapsulate his incredible journey. After 37 remarkable years as a filmmaker, and 5 worldwide film distribution deals, Kevin now uses his gifts as a published author to share inspirational stories. His motion pictures have premiered at prestigious film festivals including Sundance, Cannes, and various European film festivals, showcasing his talent on an international stage.

With his latest release, "The Gabardine Gang," and his five best-selling books in 2024, "HYSOMETRICS," "Indie Filmmaking in the REAL WORLD," "Hold the Power," "The Handshake around the World," and "The Lost Art of Logical Thinking," Kevin continues to inspire and motivate readers around the world. His diverse range of topics reflects his multifaceted experiences and wisdom gained throughout his life.

Earning the moniker "Life Warrior," Kevin stands as a shining example of the human capacity to overcome any adversity. His unwillingness to ever quit or back down, no matter the obstacles faced, is a testament to the motto he lives by: "A Life Warrior is willing to do whatever it takes to overcome life's challenges."

Kevin's journey has not been linear or easy. But through perseverance, inner strength, and an unbreakable warrior spirit forged in both military service and personal trials, he has overcome obstacles that would have defeated lesser men. Though battered and bruised, Kevin stands tall as a shining example of human potential. His story is one of courage, resilience, and the power of embracing life's challenges with an open heart.

Kevin has used visualization techniques countless times throughout his career, a skill he honed during his time in the USAF and later applied to various aspects of his life.

Many of his film projects were shot in his head long before filming began. During his time in the industry, Kevin has used visualization to produce movies, TV shows, documentaries, music videos, and even as an author. Before his career in film, he was a successful powerlifter who used 'visualization' and 'positive thinking' techniques when competing. To this day, visualization remains a tool Kevin uses regularly. Kevin lives by the motto, "If you can see it, you can do it." After a remarkable 37-year career as a filmmaker and video producer, Kevin now wields the mighty pen to craft captivating stories in the form of books, drawing inspiration from his diverse life experiences, including his military service and his journey through the world of international cinema.

INTRODUCTION
THE POWER OF WEIRDNESS

What is weirdness? At its core, weirdness is a deviation from the norm, a departure from the expected. It's that quirky behavior, unusual thought process, or unique perspective that sets someone apart from the crowd. But weirdness is far more than just being different for the sake of it. It's a powerful force that has shaped human progress, driven innovation, and given birth to some of the most remarkable achievements in history.

Throughout time, society has often viewed weirdness with suspicion or ridicule. The "weird" person was the outsider, the misfit, the one who didn't quite fit in. But as our understanding of human psychology and creativity has evolved, so too has our belief of weirdness. What was once seen as a liability is now increasingly recognized as an asset, particularly in fields that prize innovation and original thinking.

HISTORICAL CONTEXT: WEIRD GENIUSES WHO CHANGED THE WORLD

History is replete with examples of individuals whose "weirdness" was integral to their genius. Let's consider a few:

1. **Nikola Tesla:** This brilliant inventor was known for his eccentric behaviors, including an obsession with the number 3 and a phobia of pearls. Yet his "weird" mind gave us alternating current electricity, among numerous other innovations.

2. **Albert Einstein:** Beyond his revolutionary scientific theories, Einstein was known for his quirky habits. He rarely wore socks, claimed to think better with his feet in freezing water, and often forgot to eat during intense periods of work.

3. **Vincent van Gogh:** The post-impressionist painter's mental health struggles and unusual behaviors (like allegedly eating paint and cutting off

his own ear) were intertwined with his artistic genius.

4. **Emily Dickinson:** The reclusive poet rarely left her room in later life and was known for wearing only white clothes. Her unconventional lifestyle was matched by her innovative approach to poetry.

5. **Steve Jobs:** The Apple co-founder was known for his "reality distortion field," unconventional thinking, and quirky habits like soaking his feet in toilet water to relieve stress.

These individuals, and many others like them, prove that weirdness and exceptional ability often go hand in hand. Their unique perspectives and unconventional approaches allowed them to see possibilities that others missed, driving progress in their respective fields.

THE PSYCHOLOGY OF WEIRDNESS

From a psychological perspective, weirdness is a complex and multifaceted concept. It's not a clinical term, but rather a social construct that varies across cultures and time periods. What's considered weird in one context might be perfectly normal in another.

Dr. David Weeks, a Scottish clinical neuropsychologist, conducted a comprehensive study on eccentricity (a term often used interchangeably with weirdness) in the 1980s. His research, culminating in the book "Eccentrics: A Study of Sanity and Strangeness," offered valuable insights into the nature of weirdness:

1. **Creativity:** Weeks found that eccentric individuals were highly creative, with a strong drive to create and invent.
2. **Curiosity:** "Weird" people showed an insatiable curiosity about the world around them.
3. **Idealism:** Many eccentrics were driven by a desire to make the world a better place.
4. **Obsessive Interests:** Weird individuals often had intense, focused interests or hobbies.
5. **Non-conformity:** They showed a general disregard for fitting in with social norms.
6. **High Intelligence:** On average, eccentrics scored higher on IQ tests than the general population.

7. **Health:** Surprisingly, Weeks found that eccentric individuals tended to be healthier and live longer than their "normal" counterparts.

These findings suggest that weirdness, far from being a handicap, can be associated with many positive traits and outcomes.

WEIRDNESS AND CREATIVITY: A POWERFUL CONNECTION

One of the most significant aspects of weirdness is its strong link to creativity. Numerous studies have shown a correlation between unconventional thinking (a hallmark of weirdness) and creative ability.

A 2017 study published in the journal "Personality and Individual Differences" found that people who were ranked as "weird" by their peers also scored higher on measures of creative potential. The researchers suggested that the ability to think in unusual ways - a key component of weirdness - is also crucial for creative problem-solving and innovation.

Another study, published in the "Journal of Personality and Social Psychology" in 2012, found that individuals who had lived abroad and experienced diverse cultures (a form of "weird" experience in itself) showed enhanced creativity and professional success. This suggests that exposure to "weird" or unfamiliar situations can boost creative thinking.

The connection between weirdness and creativity makes sense when we consider what creativity really is. At its core, creativity is about making novel connections, seeing patterns where others don't, and imagining new possibilities. These are all traits that weird thinkers excel at.

WEIRDNESS IN THE WORKPLACE

In the past, being labeled as "weird" in a professional context was often seen as a liability. However, as the business world increasingly values innovation and out-of-the-box thinking, weirdness is becoming an asset.

A 2018 study by management consulting firm McKinsey & Company found that diversity of thought – including having team members with unconventional perspectives – was a key factor in driving innovation in businesses. Companies with more diverse leadership teams were more likely to report above-average profitability.

Similarly, a 2017 report by Deloitte emphasized the importance of "diversity of thinking" in driving innovation and managing complex problems in the workplace. The report suggested that organizations should actively seek out individuals with different thinking styles, including those who might be considered "weird" by conventional standards.

These findings are changing how businesses approach hiring and team building. Many forward-thinking companies are now actively seeking out "weird" thinkers to drive innovation and provide fresh perspectives.

THE NEUROSCIENCE OF WEIRDNESS

Recent advances in neuroscience have provided intriguing insights into the brain activity of "weird" or highly creative individuals. A 2018 study published in the Proceedings of the National Academy of Sciences found that highly creative people have more connections between two areas of the brain that are typically at odds: the default network (associated with spontaneous thinking and imagination) and the control network (associated with focus and goal-directed behavior).

This unique neural architecture may explain why weird thinkers are able to generate unusual ideas (via the default network) while also having the cognitive control to channel these ideas into productive output.

Another study, published in the journal "Social Cognitive and Affective Neuroscience" in 2016, found that individuals with elevated levels of "openness to experience" (a personality trait often associated with weirdness) had more active imaginations and more vivid sensory experiences. This heightened sensory processing could contribute to the unique perspectives and ideas that characterize weird thinking.

WEIRDNESS AND MENTAL HEALTH

It's important to note that while weirdness can be a positive trait, it can sometimes be associated with mental health challenges. The line between eccentricity and mental illness can be blurry, and many great thinkers throughout history have struggled with mental health issues.

However, research suggests that embracing one's weirdness can actually be beneficial for mental health. A 2017 study published in the Journal of Research in Personality found that self-acceptance – including acceptance of one's quirks and unusual traits - was strongly linked to positive mental health outcomes.

Moreover, the ability to think differently and challenge norms – key aspects of weirdness – can be protective factors against certain mental health issues. For example, a 2019 study in the journal "Frontiers in Psychology" found that cognitive flexibility (the ability to adapt one's thinking to new situations) was associated with greater resilience to stress and lower levels of anxiety and depression.

WEIRDNESS ACROSS CULTURES

It's crucial to recognize that what's considered "weird" varies significantly across cultures. What might be seen as strange or eccentric in one society could be perfectly normal in another. This cultural relativity of weirdness highlights its subjective nature and underscores the importance of diversity in human societies.

Anthropologists have long studied how diverse cultures view and value unusual behaviors or perspectives. In some societies, individuals who would be considered "weird" in Western contexts are revered as shamans, healers, or visionaries. This cross-cultural perspective reminds us that weirdness is not an inherent quality, but a social construct that reflects the norms and values of a particular culture.

EMBRACING WEIRDNESS: A PATH TO AUTHENTICITY

In recent years, there's been a growing movement towards embracing weirdness as a path to authenticity and self-actualization. This shift is reflected in popular culture, self-help literature, and even corporate messaging that encourages people to "be yourself" and celebrate what makes them unique.

Psychologists have long recognized the importance of authenticity for mental health and well-being. Carl Rogers, one of the founders of humanistic psychology, emphasized the importance of the "true self" in his theory of personality development. According to Rogers, psychological health is achieved when there's congruence between one's true self and one's outward behavior.

In this context, embracing one's weirdness can be seen as a form of self-actualization – a way of aligning one's outer expression with one's inner truth. By accepting and celebrating their unique qualities, individuals can achieve greater self-acceptance, confidence, and overall life satisfaction.

THE VALUE OF WEIRDNESS IN A CHANGING WORLD

As we navigate an increasingly complex and rapidly changing world, the value of weirdness has never been clearer. The challenges we face – from climate change to global pandemics to technological disruption - require new ways of thinking and innovative solutions. Weird thinkers, with their ability to see things differently and challenge established norms, are uniquely positioned to contribute to solving these problems.

Moreover, in an age of artificial intelligence and automation, uniquely human traits like creativity, emotional intelligence, and out-of-the-box thinking are becoming increasingly valuable. Weirdness, with its strong links to creativity and innovation, may well be a key factor in still being relevant and valuable in the workforce of the future.

Ultimately, weirdness is not just about being different for the sake of it. It's about embracing our unique perspectives, challenging assumptions, and pushing boundaries. It's about having the courage to think differently and the conviction to act on those thoughts. In a world that often pressures us to conform, embracing our weirdness is a radical act of self-acceptance and a powerful catalyst for change.

As we move forward, it's clear that we don't just need to tolerate weirdness – we need to actively cultivate and celebrate it. Because in the end, it's the weird ones – the misfits, the rebels, the round pegs in square holes - who are most likely to change the world.

CHAPTER 1
EMBRACE YOU

L isten up, because this is the only thing you need to remember from this entire book: being a quirky oddball is your secret superpower.

People don't fall in love with your sameness; they fall for your eccentricities. Your weirdness is your differentiator, the spark that ignites curiosity and makes others want to dive deeper into your world.

Picture this: You're in a sea of job applications, all blending into a monotonous blur. But then, there's you – the technicolor splash in a grayscale world. Your oddness is what makes the recruiter's eyes widen, what causes them to lean in and think, "Now this is someone I need to meet."

But it's not just about standing out in a stack of resumes. Your uniqueness is the key that unlocks doors you never even knew existed. It's the conversation starter that turns a mundane networking event into a life-changing opportunity. It's the spark that ignites passionate discussions and forges deep connections.

Imagine you're at an event, surrounded by people asking for selfies with a celebrity. But you? You're the one who strikes up a conversation about the weirdest conspiracy theory you've both heard, creating a memorable moment that'll stick long after the Instagram likes fades away. That's the power of embracing your quirks – it creates authentic, unforgettable experiences.

Your strangeness is the bridge that connects you to people who seem to have nothing in common with you. It's the "who the hell is that?" question that changes the trajectory of your life, opening doors you never knew existed. In a world where everyone is trying to fit in, your willingness to stand out makes you magnetic.

When you embrace your quirks and start believing in your unique powers, that's when the magic happens.

That's when people rally behind your cause, not because you're odd or unusual, but because you're unapologetically you. You become a beacon for others, a living, breathing invitation for them to embrace their own weirdness.

Think about it – every great innovation, every change in thinking, every cultural revolution started with someone who dared to be different. The Wright brothers were laughed at for thinking humans could fly. Einstein was considered a poor student because his mind worked differently. Lady Gaga was told she was too weird for pop music. But it was their weirdness, their unique perspective, that allowed them to change the world.

Remember those things that made you feel like an outcast in high school? Guess what? They're your superpowers now. That obscure knowledge about ancient civilizations? It could be the foundation of your next big idea. Your uncanny ability to find patterns in chaos? That's a skill many companies would kill for. Your bizarre sense of humor? It could be the trademark of your personal brand.

Accepting your strangeness isn't just liberating; it's downright thrilling. We don't do it for fame or fortune, but for the freedom to be ourselves and to pave the way for others to do the same. When you embrace your weirdness, you give others permission to do the same. You create a ripple effect of authenticity that can transform communities, workplaces, and even societies.

Being different isn't just okay – it's powerful. Once you accept who you are, quirks and all, you'll discover a wellspring of strength you never knew you had. You'll be a better worker because you'll bring unique solutions to the table. You'll be a better friend because you'll have the courage to be vulnerable and authentic. You'll be a better lover because you'll know your worth and won't settle for less. You'll be a better human being because you'll have the confidence to stand up for what you believe in, even when it's not popular.

Weird people don't just live good lives – they make history. They're the ones who challenge the status quo, who ask "why not?" instead of "why?", who dare to dream of a different world and then make it happen. They're the inventors, the artists, the leaders who shape our culture and push humanity forward.

So go ahead, **embrace your weirdness**. Let your freak flag fly high and proud. The world is waiting for the unique flavor that only you can bring to the table. Your quirks, your passions, your peculiarities – they're not flaws to be hidden, they're gifts to be shared. In a world of copycats and conformists, your weirdness is your greatest asset. Use it wisely, use it boldly, and watch as it transforms not just your life, but the lives of those around you.

Remember, in the grand tapestry of life, it's the irregular threads that create the most interesting patterns. So be that bright, bold, beautifully bizarre thread. The world needs your weirdness more than you know.

CHAPTER 2
WHO WANTS TO BE NORMAL?

L et's face it – we all have our quirks. No matter your background, personality, or how much of a public figure you are, it's undeniable that we all do things others might find strange. Even celebrities, those seemingly perfect beings, have personal eccentricities that leave us scratching our heads.

Sometimes these are minor oddities they've grown accustomed to over time. Other times, they're habits born from superstition, dedication, or their relentless pursuit of success or beauty. Whatever the case, these nuggets of weirdness never fail to captivate us.

The truth is no one really wants to be normal. Some of the world's biggest role models and most successful individuals have achieved greatness by embracing what makes them unique. They've turned their oddities into their trademarks, their eccentricities into their brand. Take Salvador Dali, for instance. When you think of surrealism, you probably picture Dali with his waxed mustache. His life was as bizarre and weird as his paintings. Beyond driving around in a car filled with cauliflowers and strolling through Paris with an anteater (yes, really), there was something even stranger.

Dali treated his muse and love of his life, Gala, like a goddess. He bought her a castle and was only allowed to visit his wife with a signed invitation. Talk about taking "absence makes the heart grow fonder" to a whole new level! But it was this very strangeness that made Dali unforgettable, that cemented his place in art history.

Or consider Leo Tolstoy, the Russian literary giant. Tolstoy didn't just write historically exact works; he became historically significant while still alive – and fully embracing his incredibly unique personality.

Despite coming from the highest echelons of society, Tolstoy eventually began to question the morals of the world he lived in and started carving his own path. He became a vegetarian, began a rigorous daily practice, and scorned the appearance of a wealthy man. He started wearing peasant clothing and shoes he had manufactured himself, despite his lack of cobbling skills. Talk about commitment to a cause!

But Tolstoy's eccentricities weren't just personal quirks – they were a reflection of his values, his quest for authenticity, and his desire to live according to his principles. His weirdness wasn't just tolerated; it became an integral part of his legacy.

Throughout history, countless individuals have changed the world by not shying away from what made them unique, different, and totally themselves. These people didn't just survive; they thrived. And it wasn't just because of their talent. They flourished because they embraced a side of themselves that nurtured their talent and let it shine like a supernova.

Think about Albert Einstein, with his wild hair and habit of not wearing socks. Or Nikola Tesla, who was obsessed with the number 3 and would walk around a block three times before entering a building. These weren't just harmless eccentricities – they were part of what made these geniuses who they were.

In more recent times, consider Steve Jobs and his black turtleneck uniform, or Mark Zuckerberg's grey t-shirt routine. These aren't just fashion choices – they're statements about priorities, about focusing energy on what really matters rather than on trivial decisions.

Who wants to be normal? Not the game-changers, the history-makers, the ones who leave an indelible mark on the world. **Normal is for those who are content with**

blending in. But you? You're meant to stand out. You're meant to embrace your weirdness and use it to change the world.

Normal doesn't push boundaries. Normal doesn't ask "what if?" Normal doesn't revolutionize industries or create masterpieces. Normal is safe, but it's also stagnant. Your weirdness, on the other hand, is dynamic. It's the force that propels you to try new things, to see the world from a different angle, to solve problems in ways no one else has thought of.

Embracing your weirdness isn't just about accepting yourself – it's about giving yourself permission to be great. It's about recognizing that the very things that make you different are the things that make you valuable, innovative, and irreplaceable.

The next time someone calls you weird, thank them. Wear it as a badge of honor.

Because in a world that's constantly changing, that's facing unprecedented challenges and opportunities, we don't need more normal. We need weirder. We need your weird.

Remember, every great idea, every revolutionary concept, every change in thinking in human history started with someone who dared to be different. Someone who looked at the world not as it was, but as it could be. Someone who wasn't afraid to be called weird.

That someone could be you. **Be weird. Nurture it**. Share it with the world. Because who knows? Your brand of weird might be exactly what the world needs right now.

CHAPTER 3

BEING WEIRD MAKES YOU AUTHENTIC

Listen up because this is important: Weirdness is not just okay – it's downright fantastic. It's what sets us apart while simultaneously connecting us to the very essence of humanity. We often forget that what makes us unique are the things we're passionate about, and the depths to which that passion can go.

We tend to overlook the fact that our interests, whether they're devouring books, dominating at Scrabble, or crafting mind-bending comic books, are valid and absolutely amazing. These aren't just hobbies; they're the building blocks of our authentic selves.

Authenticity is like a superpower in today's world of carefully curated social media personas and corporate-speak. When you're truly authentic, people can feel it. They're drawn to it. Why? Because authenticity is rare, and it's refreshing.

In a world where everyone is trying to be someone else, being yourself is revolutionary.

Now, let's talk about imitation. It's how we humans learn to do things. We've always done it, and we'll keep doing it. It's the most surefire way to improve your technique and understand the ins and outs of anything. Many people imitate those they admire when they're crafting their own persona.

But here's the kicker – while we're busy imitating, we're also discovering who we truly are. And sometimes, we learn to be someone other than ourselves. We look at the successful people, those who followed the rules, and we start chipping away at the parts of our lives that don't fit the mold. Slowly but surely, we lose our unique character quirks and personality.

This is where the danger lies. When we start to erase our weirdness in an attempt to fit in, we're not just losing our quirks – we're losing our authenticity. We're losing the very thing that makes us special, that makes us valuable, that makes us.

Then we start wondering: Can we still listen to polka music or create rock operas if we want to be star employees and rake in the big bucks? Or, if we really want to make it in a creative field, do we have to shoehorn our work into the mainstream?

The answer is a resounding no. In fact, it's often the weird, the different, the authentic that rises to the top. Think about the most memorable people you know – chances are, they're not the ones who blend in perfectly. They're the ones who stand out, who have that special something that you can't quite put your finger on.

We either consciously or subconsciously repeat this to ourselves, and we begin to feel embarrassed or ashamed of the way we were before we stuffed ourselves into a neat little box. But this box isn't just uncomfortable – it's stifling. It's limiting our potential, our creativity, our ability to connect with others on a deep, meaningful level.

But it wasn't always like this. Remember when you were a kid? You used to let your freak flag fly with reckless abandon. You'd run around in pink storm trooper gear, fully embracing every quirky aspect of yourself. You didn't care what anyone thought – you were too busy being you.

As we grow older, we learn to tuck that side away, to find a place to lock it up so we can pretend it was never there. But here's the truth: that weirdness, that uniqueness, that authenticity – it's your superpower. And it's time to break it out of its cage.

Being authentic doesn't mean you never change or grow. It doesn't mean you can't adapt to different situations. What it does mean is that at your core, you stay true to who you are. You don't compromise your values, your passions, or your unique perspective on the world.

When you embrace your weirdness, you're embracing your authenticity. You're saying to the world, "This is me, in all my glory, with all my quirks and passions and peculiarities." And you know what? The world needs that. The world needs you – the real you, not some watered-down, sanitized version that you think will be more acceptable.

Your authenticity is what will draw people to you. It's what will make you stand out in a job interview, what will make your art resonate with people, what will make your ideas innovative and groundbreaking. Your authenticity is what will make you unforgettable.

Let your weird shine through in everything you do. Be proud of your quirks, your unique interests, your unique way of seeing the world. Because that's not just who you are – it's your greatest strength. It's what makes you authentic, and in a world of copies and imitations, authenticity is priceless.

CHAPTER 4
BEING UNIQUE MAKES YOU CREATIVE

Here's the cold, hard truth: **You'll never be able to embrace creativity if you try to march in lockstep with what you perceive to be the mainstream**. If you're constantly trying to mirror the worker in the cubicle next to you who always says and does the "right" thing – rather than the real thing – you're stifling your creative potential.

The best solutions, ideas, and products don't appear from conventional thinking. Some people might call this kind of thinking weird, but it's just unique, authentic, and can make you a powerhouse in all levels of society.

Creativity isn't about following a set of rules or sticking to proven norms. It's about breaking those rules, challenging those norms, and seeing the world in a way that no one else does. And guess what? That's exactly what your weirdness allows you to do.

The ideas that come from being unique are the result of a creative twist that only a completely devoted freak could have devised. That's what you need to aim for. If you put a stop to it, you'll be suffocating whatever chance you had to be truly extraordinary.

Think about some of the most creative people in history. Vincent van Gogh was considered strange and unstable in his time, but his unique vision revolutionized art. Nikola Tesla was seen as eccentric and obsessive, but his weird ideas gave us alternating current electricity. Steve Jobs was often described as difficult and unconventional, but his unique approach to technology changed the way we communicate.

These people weren't creative despite their weirdness – they were creative because of it. Their unique perspectives allowed them to see possibilities that others couldn't even imagine.

If you try to transform yourself into a stranger, someone you don't recognize when you look in the mirror and see gray where there used to be brilliant color, you'll end up hurting yourself eventually. It's going to crush you. You'll be suppressing not just your personality, but your creative potential.

You'll begin to lose any sense of worth in your life, and you won't feel comfortable in your own skin. That's not the way to live. It's not the way to be. It's not a sustainable way to exist. And it's certainly not the way to unlock your creative potential.

When you begin to lose the elements of yourself that give you a zest for life, that fire will eventually die out. And trust me, you don't want to be left with just ashes where your passion used to burn bright. Creativity needs fuel, and that fuel is your unique perspective, your weird ideas, your unusual way of seeing the world.

Let your creativity flow from the wellspring of your authentic self. Because that's where the magic happens – that's where you'll find ideas and solutions that no one else could possibly conceive. That's your superpower, and it's time to use it.

Don't be afraid to bring your weird ideas to the table. Don't hesitate to approach problems from an angle that might seem strange to others. Your unique perspective might be exactly what's needed to solve that seemingly unsolvable problem, to create that revolutionary product, to author that unforgettable story.

Remember, creativity isn't about being right all the time. It's about being willing to be wrong, to take risks, to try things that might not work. And who's better equipped to do that than someone who's already comfortable with being different?

Your weirdness gives you the freedom to think outside the box because you've never really been in the box to begin with. Use that freedom. Explore those wild ideas. Follow those strange trains of thought. You never know where they might lead you.

In a world that's facing unprecedented challenges, we need creative solutions more than ever. We need people who can look at old problems with new eyes, who can imagine possibilities that others can't see. We need your weirdness, your uniqueness, your creativity.

So let your freak flag fly. Embrace your quirks. Use your unique perspective to fuel your creativity. Because the world doesn't need another cookie-cutter thinker – it needs you, in all your weird, wonderful, creative glory.

CHAPTER 5

YOU LOSE A LOT WHEN YOU'RE NOT AUTHENTIC

L isten up, because this is crucial: People will react when you aren't trying to hide your true nature. When you're showing authenticity rather than a phony persona, that's when you'll be able to reach out and connect with other people on a deeper level.

It's about allowing the world to see the genuine person underneath your skin rather than the image you wish to project. Everything we do stands for a distinct aspect of our personality. But every part is always based on something true, something that comes from our core self.

When you're not authentic, you're not just losing a part of yourself – you're losing opportunities. Opportunities to connect, to create, to inspire, to lead. You're losing the chance to make a real, lasting impact on the world around you.

Think about it. When was the last time you were profoundly moved by someone who seemed fake or inauthentic? Chances are, it's been a while. That's because we're hardwired to respond to authenticity. We can sense it, even if we can't always put our finger on what it is.

People you genuinely admire are well aware of their quirks and passions. This is a proven fact. Every creative is a passionate freak, whether they're entrepreneurs and founders, comic book artists, or speed metal bands. If they weren't, the world would be a far less colorful place.

Think about it. Benjamin Franklin, Michael Bloomberg, Steve Jobs, Robin Williams, and Gertrude Stein – all motivated, authentic, and – to some – weird individuals. And it was those unique and authentic personalities that motivated them to do things that have changed millions, if not billions, of people.

These people didn't succeed despite their quirks – they succeeded because of them. Their authenticity allowed them to connect with people on a deep level, to inspire loyalty and admiration, to create things that resonated with people's souls.

You don't have to be a full-time artist or a founder to embrace your authenticity. But it would be foolish to dismiss their successes and the things they were able to carry out as a result of their passions. It's a clear sign that adhering to and sustaining your unique qualities is a worthwhile investment.

When you're not authentic, you're constantly playing a role. And let me tell you, that's exhausting. It's mentally and emotionally draining to always be on guard, always trying to be what you think others want you to be. When you're authentic, on the other hand, you free up all that energy to actually live your life, to pursue your passions, to connect with others.

We want to celebrate our personality traits not just because it fosters authenticity, but also because when we work and live from our actual selves, we build a richer, stronger, more dynamic, and varied environment around us. This means adding the distinct flavor of our particular abilities, character, and values to our work. It involves giving others the freedom to be themselves in the face of your entire presence. It means the world becomes a truer mirror of who we are, rather than who we believe we should be.

When you're not authentic, you're robbing the world of your unique gifts. You're denying others the chance to know the real you, to receive help from your unique perspective, to be inspired by your particular brand of weirdness. You're creating a world that's a little less colorful, a little less interesting, a little less authentic.

Hold a mirror up to every beautiful part of your strangeness. Reconnect with your whole self and allow us to see every abstract, weirdly shaped, metallic rainbow part of it. Because when you're not authentic, you're not just losing a part of yourself – you're depriving the world of the unique gift that only you can offer.

Remember, authenticity isn't just about being true to yourself. It's about creating a world where everyone feels free to be who they truly are. And that starts with you embracing every quirky, wonderful aspect of your personality. So go ahead, let your freak flag fly. The world is waiting for the real you.

When you're authentic, you inspire others to be authentic too.

You create a ripple effect of genuineness that can transform relationships, workplaces, and communities. You become a beacon of truth in a world that often feels fake and superficial.

Don't underestimate the power of your authenticity. It's not just about you – it's about the impact you can have on the world around you. When you're true to yourself, you give others permission to do the same. You create spaces where people feel safe to be themselves, to express their ideas, to pursue their passions.

Show your weirdness, your quirks, your unique perspective. Don't hide them away or try to smooth them out. They're not flaws to be fixed – they're the very things that make you valuable, interesting, and irreplaceable.

Remember, you lose a lot when you're not authentic. You lose the chance to form deep, meaningful connections. You lose opportunities to innovate and create. You lose the ability to inspire others. But most importantly, you lose yourself. And that's a price that's simply too high to pay.

CHAPTER 6
THINK OUTSIDE THE BOX

Here's a fact that might blow your mind: **people who think outside the box and embrace being different get stuff done**. They develop disruptive businesses, modern technologies, movements, and push others to think differently. All our generation's incredible advances wouldn't exist if weirdos didn't exist to question the status quo.

Unleash your inner oddball to realize our full creative potential? And what can we do to be a bit weirder, a little better at thinking freely, a little less tuned in to societal and cultural expectations? Because the answers to these questions show that being a bit odder may help us all become a lot more creative.

The average person will react to situations quickly based on what they've been instructed by those in charge. A distinctive or "weird" individual, on the other hand, is less inclined to heed authority or grasp social norms. Creative people live in a hazier, fluid, ethereal environment, and although a highly original person may seem unusual or peculiar to others, it's precisely this sort of social oddity that leads to creative breakthroughs.

Think about it. If everyone thought the same way, we'd still be living in caves. It's the people who dared to think differently, to challenge assumptions, to ask "why not?" instead of "why?" who have driven human progress. And guess what? Those people were probably considered weird in their time.

People who are open to new experiences and have the capacity to challenge the current quo might interpret their surroundings in novel ways. Looking for the unexpected and venturing outside of your own experience leads to creativity. Being strange to some is just being open to new experiences and ideas.

But how do you open yourself up even more and push your creative and think-outside-the-box mentality? Simple, you practice what you preach. It's not enough to just accept your weirdness – you need to actively cultivate it, to push yourself to explore new ideas, to seek out experiences that challenge your assumptions.

It has long been questioned whether creativity can be taught, yet it's commonly agreed that being open to new experiences is a creative attribute that can be cultivated. There's no excuse if all you need to be more creative is to go out of your comfort zone!

Patronize a different ethnic restaurant, learn a language, do the hardest crossword puzzle you can find, read a challenging book – any experience, as long as it's new and beyond your comfort zone, can broaden your thinking and make you more creative. Some may label you as odd, but genuinely creative individuals understand that being open to new experiences and trying new things is one of the greatest ways to create fresh, unique connections and generate innovative ideas.

Remember, each of us has had a unique combination of events that have shaped us into the people we are today. People from unusual origins tend to be the most creative since they have a distinct view of the world. Your unique experiences, your quirks, your peculiar interests – they're not just random oddities. They're the ingredients that make up your unique perspective, and that perspective is invaluable.

Surprise occurrences and unusual experiences might range from living abroad to experiencing a family tragedy, and they all give what psychologists call "cognitive flexibility," which boosts your creativity. So don't shy away from the weird, the unexpected, the challenging. Embrace these experiences as opportunities to expand your mind and fuel your creativity.

In some ways, we all come from strange backgrounds. Nobody was raised the same way we were. And no one else sees the world the same way we do. Although it may seem overwhelming to understand how much some people have gone through, everyone has experienced, done, imagined, or felt something completely unique –

something which no one else has ever gone through. That's quite incredible. As a result, some people are able to be creative because of their ability to harness their background and the distinct viewpoint it has given them.

The secret to unlocking your innermost creativity is to reflect and get to the core of what makes you unique. Finding out what makes you unique might be challenging, but once you discover it, you have a clear path to creativity because all you have to do is perceive the world through your unique perspective, which is as simple as being yourself.

How do you discover what makes you unique? Try finding yourself by asking questions such as, "What am I particularly good at?" "What are my favorite things?" "What do I find appealing?" "What do I find repulsive?" "How would my friends characterize me?" "How would I characterize myself?" "What would I do if I had an hour to myself? A free day? A month off? A year off?" These kinds of inquiries dive deep into what makes you tick and what your priorities are.

By getting to know yourself better, you'll be able to figure out what kind of craziness you can bring to the table, whether in a group or on your own. Although some people come from more unusual backgrounds than others, we all have a unique set of experiences that no one else has. We all have our own unique perspective on the world, and we all have the power to communicate it. Being unique, therefore, is a matter of perspective. We're all different.

The distinction in our creative potential is how much we've been able to capitalize on our own brand of weirdness. So go ahead, embrace your quirks, think outside the box, and let your unique perspective shine. The world is waiting for your brand of creativity.

Remember, thinking outside the box isn't just about being different for the sake of being different. It's about approaching problems from new angles, seeing connections that others miss, and having the courage to propose solutions that might seem crazy at first. Your weirdness gives you a unique vantage point – use it to your advantage.

Don't be afraid to bring your weird ideas to the table. Even if they don't work out, they might spark a conversation or inspire someone else to think differently. In a world that's facing unprecedented challenges, we need all the out-of-the-box thinking we can get.

Use your weird self to fuel your creativity. Let it inspire you to think in ways that no one else does. Because who knows? Your brand of weird might just be exactly what the world needs right now.

CHAPTER 7

TAP YOUR WEIRDNESS POTENTIAL

Understanding what it means to be strange is accepting that we all have the ability for oddness. And, although this isn't always a compliment, it most certainly is when it comes to innovation.

Strange people are trailblazers. A crazy person's brain does not exclude ideas just because they don't seem to be absolutely vital at the moment. If Steve Jobs had done that, we might not be holding smartphones in our hands right now. Your weird ideas, the ones that seem too out there, too impractical, too strange – they might just be the seeds of the next big innovation.

Everything we go through, no matter how typical or strange our lives seem to be, is fuel for future creation and should therefore be stored, unpacked, and tinkered with until all of these concepts combine into fresh, creative ideas. Keeping an open mind to new experiences is a terrific approach to add to your creative arsenal. Another approach is to recognize your distinct point of view on the world. And, although collective thinking may be detrimental to creativity, the capacity to seek out other odd people is one of the most effective methods to generate new ideas.

So go out there and proudly wear your weird badge. Besides, why would you want to be normal when it's the oddballs that have the power to alter the world? Normal doesn't change things. Normal doesn't push boundaries. Normal doesn't create revolutions or spark movements. Weird does.

Remember, your weirdness is not a liability – it's an asset. It's the key that unlocks doors to innovation, creativity, and success that others can't even see. Your unique perspective, your quirky habits, your unconventional thoughts – these are the ingredients for greatness.

Don't just accept your weirdness – celebrate it. Nurture it. Let it grow and evolve. Your weirdness potential is limitless, and it's up to you to tap into it. Who knows? Your peculiar way of looking at the world might just be the solution to a problem no one else has been able to solve.

Tapping into your weirdness potential isn't always easy. It requires courage. It requires a willingness to be vulnerable, to put yourself out there, to risk being misunderstood or ridiculed. But the potential rewards are immense. By fully embracing your weirdness, you open yourself up to innovative ideas, new connections, new possibilities that you might never have discovered otherwise.

So how do you tap into this potential? Start by giving yourself permission to be weird. Allow yourself to explore those odd ideas, those strange connections, those quirky interests that you might have been suppressing. Don't judge your thoughts or ideas – just let them flow.

Next, surround yourself with other weird people. Seek out those who think differently, who challenge the status quo, who aren't afraid to be themselves. These people can inspire you, support you, and help you see your own weirdness in a new light.

Finally, **use your weirdness as a tool**.

When you're faced with a problem, ask yourself, "How would my weird side approach this?" You might be surprised at the innovative solutions you come up with.

Remember, your weirdness is a gift. It's what makes you unique, what sets you apart from the crowd. Don't hide it away – let it shine. Because the world doesn't need more normal. **It needs more weird**. It needs more you.

So go ahead, be weird. Embrace your quirks, your oddities, your unique way of seeing the world. Tap into your weirdness potential and see where it takes you. You might just change the world in the process.

CHAPTER 8

EMBRACING YOUR WEIRD MAKES YOU MENTALLY STRONG

L isten up, because this is crucial: Being true to yourself is one of the most self-loving things you can do. If someone tells you that you're strange, you should wear that label like a badge of honor. It's not just about accepting your quirks – it's about recognizing that these very quirks are the source of your mental strength.

To be yourself, you must first understand yourself. You know what brings you joy and what your unique perspective is. Because you know yourself, you make excellent decisions. This self-awareness is the foundation of mental strength. When you're in tune with your true self, you're better equipped to handle life's challenges.

Maybe you can ride a horse like a rodeo star, play a musical instrument that most people can't even pronounce, speak a couple of obscure languages, or draw in a style that makes Picasso look mainstream. Perhaps you've traveled to countries that aren't even on most maps and experienced cultures that would blow most people's minds. These aren't just interesting facts about you – they're evidence of your courage, your curiosity, your willingness to step outside your comfort zone. And that, my friend, is mental strength in action.

Because you're not afraid to try anything out of the ordinary, you've accomplished much and are hungry to learn even more! This constant drive to explore, to learn, to grow – it's a hallmark of mental strength. It shows resilience, adaptability, and a growth mindset.

Some people are terrified to walk to a grocery store alone because they think everyone is judging them, but that's not you. Some folks can't even register for classes without their buddies holding their hands, but that's not your style; you take on whatever you want. Keep crushing it!

This independence, this ability to stand on your own two feet – it's a clear sign of mental strength.

Here's the thing: Why would you waste time gossiping about others if you don't care what they think of you? You're tolerant and open-minded because you have to be to embrace yourself fully. This ability to rise above petty judgments and accept others as they are – it's another aspect of mental strength.

It's true. **Haters will always hate. Not everyone will get your unique flavor**. But if you believe you're awesome, chances are you really are! This self-confidence, this ability to stand firm in your self-belief even in the face of criticism – that's mental strength personified.

Your friends trust you and enjoy how much fun you are because you're always authentically you, honest to the core, and not a shred of shadiness in sight. This authenticity, this ability to be true to yourself regardless of the situation – it's a powerful form of mental strength.

Because you refuse to let anyone drag you down, you have control over your emotions. You're one of the most mentally strong people you know. And you'll only feel more powerful when you truly embrace who you are and why you are. Don't be afraid of your personality, your quirks, your unique nature. In fact, you need to look at it as your secret weapon, a tool to make yourself more confident and surer that you really are unlike anyone else – and that's not good, it's freaking fantastic.

Embracing your weirdness isn't always easy. It takes courage to stand out in a world that often prizes conformity. But every time you choose to be true to yourself, every time you let your freak flag fly, you're building mental strength. You're telling the world – and yourself – that you're worthy just as you are.

This mental strength manifests in many ways. It's the resilience to bounce back from setbacks, the courage to take risks, the confidence to express your ideas even when they're unconventional. It's the ability to laugh at yourself, to admit when you're wrong, to keep going when things get tough.

Embrace your weird. Let it fuel your mental strength. Because in a world that's constantly changing, that's full of challenges and uncertainties, mental strength is a superpower. And your weirdness? That's your unique way of tapping into that power.

Remember, mental strength isn't about never feeling weak or scared or unsure. It's about feeling all those things and moving forward anyway. It's about being true to yourself even when it's hard. It's about embracing your weird, wonderful self and using that as a source of strength.

So go ahead, be weird. Be strong. Be you. The world needs your unique brand of weirdness more than you know.

CHAPTER 9

WEIRDNESS MAKES YOU IRREPLACEABLE: THE UNFAIR ADVANTAGE OF BEING WEIRD

Alright, listen up, because this is where it gets really good. By now, you've hopefully embraced the fact that you're a bit different from other people. You know you're not like everyone else, and you never will be. And you know what? That's not just okay – it's your secret weapon.

Here's the thing: your weirdness isn't just some quirky personality trait. It's your ticket to becoming irreplaceable. Yeah, you heard that right. In a world full of cookie-cutter corporate drones and Instagram influencers all trying to look the same, your weirdness is what makes you stand out like a unicorn at a horse show.

Think about it. In your job, who's the person everyone remembers? It's not the guy who always plays it safe and follows every rule to the letter. It's the one who comes up with those crazy ideas that just might work. It's the person who sees connections that no one else does. That's you, my weird friend.

Your unique perspective? That's pure gold. While everyone else is approaching problems the same old way, you're coming at it from an angle they've never even considered. That's how innovation happens. That's how you become the person they can't afford to lose.

And it's not just about work. In your personal life, your weirdness is what draws people to you. Sure, some folks might not get you, but the ones who do? They become your ride-or-die friends. They're the ones who appreciate you for exactly who you are, quirks and all.

You know why? Because you're interesting! You're not spouting the same old small talk at parties. You're the one telling fascinating stories about that obscure hobby of yours or sharing mind-blowing facts that no one else knows. You're the one people remember long after the party's over.

But here's the real kicker: your weirdness makes you adaptable. Yeah, you heard me right. See, you've spent your whole life being a bit different, right? That means you're used to navigating situations that aren't designed for you. You're comfortable with being uncomfortable. Our world is changing faster than ever, that's a superpower.

Normal people freak out when things don't go according to plan. But you? You thrive on it. Change doesn't scare you; it excites you. It's a chance to flex those weird muscles of yours and come up with solutions no one else would think of.

And let's talk about creativity for a second. Normal is boring. Normal doesn't push boundaries. Normal doesn't create art that moves people or start revolutions or invent the next important thing. Weird does. Your weird brain makes connections that other people don't. It sees beauty where others see chaos. It finds solutions where others see dead ends.

Here's what I want you to do. I want you to stop thinking of your weirdness as something you need to tone down or hide. Instead, I want you to crank it up to eleven. Lean into it. Because your weirdness isn't just what makes you different – it's what makes you irreplaceable.

In this world where so much can be automated or outsourced, your unique brand of weird is something that can never be replicated. It's your personal stamp on everything you do. It's what makes you, well, you.

So go ahead, let your freak flag fly. Bring your weird ideas to the table. Share your unusual perspectives. Because the world doesn't need another cookie-cutter person going through the motions. It needs you, in all your weird, wonderful glory.

Remember, normal is replaceable. Weird is irreplaceable. And irreplaceable? That's unstoppable. Let's embrace your weird and watch as it makes you the most valuable person in any room you walk into. Trust me, once people get a taste of your brand of weird, they won't be able to get enough.

Now go out there and show the world just how irreplaceable you are. Because you, my weird friend, are one of a kind. And that's your superpower.

CHAPTER 10

YOUR WEIRDNESS — A PERSONAL NOTE

Well, my weird and wonderful friends, we've come to the end of our journey through the land of the strange, the quirky, and the beautifully bizarre. But before we part ways, I want to share something personal with you.

You see, I've been called weird my entire life. As a kid, I was the one with the "strange" ideas, the "odd" hobbies, the "peculiar" way of looking at the world. I heard it all – too loud, too quiet, too intense, too dreamy. For a long time, I thought there was something wrong with me. I tried to fit in, to be "normal," to sand down my rough edges until I was as smooth and unremarkable as everyone else.

But you know what? It didn't work. And thank goodness for that.

Because it was my weirdness – my unique perspective, my offbeat ideas, my unconventional approach – that led me to where I am today. It was my weirdness that allowed me to become a best-selling author, with books that have touched millions of lives around the world. It was my weirdness that inspired me to create movies that have been screened in theaters across the globe, moving audiences in ways I never could have imagined.

When I embraced my weird ideas, when I stopped trying to fit my square-peg self into the round hole of "normal," that's when the magic happened. My books resonated with people because they were different, because they came from a place of authentic weirdness. My films stood out because they didn't follow the usual formula, they were born from my unique way of seeing the world.

And that's what I want for you.

I want you to embrace your weirdness. To celebrate it. To shout it from the rooftops. Because your weirdness isn't a flaw - it's your superpower.

Your weirdness is what makes you unforgettable. It's what allows you to see solutions where others see only problems. It's what makes your art, your ideas, your very presence in this world, irreplaceable. Just as my weirdness led me to bestseller lists and silver screens, your weirdness can take you places you've never even dreamed of.

So be proud of your quirks. Use your unique perspective to show the world who you truly are. Don't hide your light under a bushel of "normalcy." Let it shine, in all its weird and wonderful glory.

Remember, the world doesn't need another cookie-cutter person going through the motions. It needs you - the real you, the weird you, **the you that only you can be**. Who knows? Your weirdness might lead you to write that breakthrough novel, direct that award-winning film, or create that world-changing innovation.

So go out there and be weird. Be proud. Be unapologetically, gloriously you.

Thank you for coming on this journey with me. Thank you for being willing to explore your weirdness, to consider the power it holds. And thank you, most of all, for being exactly who you are.

The world is waiting for your unique brand of weird. Don't keep it waiting any longer.

Now go forth, my weird and wonderful friends, and show the world what you've got. I can't wait to see what you'll create, what you'll achieve, how you'll change the world. Will your books top the bestseller lists? Will your films captivate audiences worldwide? Will your ideas revolutionize industries? I believe they will because I've seen firsthand the power of embracing one's weirdness.

Because trust me - you will make an impact. Your weirdness is your ticket to leaving your mark on the world.

Stay weird, stay wonderful, and never forget: **Your weirdness is your magic**.

Thank you for reading. Now go make some weird magic of your own. The bestseller lists, the silver screens, the world stage - they're all waiting for your unique brand of weird. Go show them what you've got.

Kevin B DiBacco
'Weird' Author

Printed in the USA
CPSIA information can be obtained
at www.ICGtesting.com
LVHW011443270824
789403LV00015B/706

By
Mary Mark Wickenhiser, FSP

BOOKS & MEDIA
Boston

Nihil Obstat: Rev. John J. Connelly, s.t.d.

Imprimatur: ✠ Bernard Cardinal Law
              Archbishop of Boston
              July 5, 2001

ISBN 0-8198-7061-7

Cover art: Tom Kinarney

Texts of the New Testament used in this work are taken from *The St. Paul Catholic Edition of the New Testament,* translated by Mark A. Wauck. Copyright © 1992, Society of St. Paul. All rights reserved.

Texts of the Psalms used in this work are translated by Manuel Miguens. Copyright © 1995, Daughters of St. Paul.

All other Old Testament Scripture quotations are from the *Christian Community Bible,* co-published by Claretian Publications and St. Paul's Publications, Philippines. Copyright © 1999, Bernardo Hurault.

"P" and Pauline are registered trademarks of the Daughters of St. Paul.

Copyright © 2002, Daughters of St. Paul

Published in the U.S.A. by Pauline Books & Media, 50 Saint Pauls Avenue, Boston MA 02130-3491.

Printed in the U.S.A.

www.pauline.org

Pauline Books & Media is the publishing house of the Daughters of St. Paul, an international congregation of women religious serving the Church with the communications media.

3 4 5 6 7   12 11 10 09 08 07

Contents

What Is a Novena?

The Catholic tradition of praying novenas has its roots in the earliest days of the Church. In the Acts of the Apostles we read that after the ascension of Jesus, the apostles returned to Jerusalem, to the upper room, where "They all devoted themselves single-mindedly to prayer, along with some women and Mary the Mother of Jesus and his brothers" (Acts 1:14). Jesus had instructed his disciples to wait for the coming of the Holy Spirit, and on the day of Pentecost, the Spirit of the Lord came to them. This prayer of the first Christian community was the first "novena." Based on this, Christians have always prayed for various needs, trusting that God both hears and answers prayer.

The word "novena" is derived from the Latin term *novem,* meaning nine. In biblical times numbers held deep symbolism for people. The number "three," for example, symbolized perfection, fullness, completeness. The number nine—three times three—symbolized perfection times perfection. Novenas developed because it was thought that—symbolically speaking—nine days represented the perfect amount of time to pray. The ancient Greeks and Romans had the custom of mourning for nine days after a death. The early Christian Church offered Mass for the deceased for nine consecutive days. During the Middle Ages novenas in preparation for solemn feasts became popular, as did novenas to particular saints.

Whether a novena is made solemnly—in a parish church in preparation for a feastday—or in the privacy of one's home, as Christians we never really pray alone. Through the waters of Baptism we have become members of the body of Christ and are thereby united to every other member of Christ's Mystical Body. When we pray, we are spiritually united with all the other members.

Just as we pray for each other while here on earth, those who have gone before us and are united with God in heaven can pray for us and intercede for us as well. We Catholics use the term "communion of saints" to refer to this exchange of spiritual help among the members of the Church on earth, those who have died and are being purified, and the saints in heaven.

While nothing can replace the celebration of Mass and the sacraments as the Church's highest form of prayer, devotions have a special place in Catholic life. Devotions such as the Stations of the Cross can help us enter into the sufferings of Jesus and give us an understanding of his personal love for us. The mysteries of the rosary can draw us into meditating on the lives of Jesus and Mary. Devotions to the saints can help us witness to our faith and encourage us in our commitment to lead lives of holiness and service as they did.

How to use this booklet

*T*he morning and evening prayers are modeled on the Liturgy of the Hours, following its pattern of psalms, scripture readings and intercessions.

We suggest that during the novena you make time in your schedule to pray the morning prayer and evening prayer. If you are able, try to also set aside a time during the day when you can pray the novena and any other particular prayer(s) you have chosen. Or you can recite the devotional prayers at the conclusion of the morning or evening prayer. What is important is to pray with expectant faith and confidence in a loving God who will answer our prayers in the way that will most benefit us. The Lord "satisfies the thirsty, and the hungry he fills with good things" (Ps 107:9).

The Archangel Raphael

We meet the Archangel Raphael, whose name means "God heals," in the Old Testament book of Tobit, written to instruct and inspire its readers.

In the story, God hears the prayers of Tobit, a devout Jew exiled in Nineveh who has been blinded by cataracts, and Sarah, a young woman in Media. She has been married seven times but on her wedding night each husband has been killed by the demon Asmodeus. The Lord sends Raphael to heal both Tobit and Sarah.

Without revealing his true identity, Raphael guides Tobit's son, Tobiah, to Media to obtain a cure for his father's blindness. While in Media, Raphael also arranges the marriage between Tobiah and Sarah, and instructs Tobiah how to drive away the evil demon. Tobiah survives the wedding night; Sarah and her family rejoice over the wondrous event and the newlyweds return home to Tobit. There,

Raphael again instructs Tobiah how to effect the cure for Tobit's blindness, and then reveals to them his identity: "I am Raphael, one of the seven holy angels who present the prayers of holy people and who stand before the glory of the Lord" (Tob 12:15). Tobit and his family praise God for the great blessings they have received through the angel Raphael.

The story of Tobit reminds us not only that the existence of angels is a belief of our Christian faith-tradition, but also that God can "send" angels to help us in our needs, although we cannot see them. Angels are servants and messengers of God who always behold the face of God (cf. Mt 18:10) and stand ready to do the Lord's bidding (cf. Ps 103:20). For this reason, artists usually depict angels with wings and flowing garments, surrounded in light. But in reality angels do not have bodies, because they are purely spiritual creatures. They are personal beings who possess intelligence and free will as we do.

Sacred Scripture presents angels performing various services for the Lord. An angel came to Mary and told her that God had chosen her to be the mother of his son. Angels heralded the birth of Jesus and announced this good news to the shepherds. Angels ministered to Jesus during his agony in the garden; angels announced Jesus' resurrection to the disciples at the empty tomb, and when Peter was imprisoned, angels came to free him.

The Archangel Raphael is regarded as the angel of joy, and is invoked as the angel of healing, the patron of travelers and bearers of the Good News, and the patron of men and women seeking a good spouse.

The feast of Saint Raphael is celebrated on September 29 together with the Archangels Michael and Gabriel.

Morning Prayer

Morning prayer is a time to give praise and thanks to God, to remind ourselves that he is the source of all beauty and goodness. Lifting one's heart and mind to God in the early hours of the day puts one's life into perspective: God is our loving Creator who watches over us with tenderness and is always ready to embrace us with his compassion and mercy.

While at prayer, try to create a prayerful atmosphere, perhaps with a burning candle to remind you that Christ is the light who illumines your daily path, an open Bible to remind you that the Lord is always present, a crucifix to remind you of the depths of God's love for you. Soft music can also contribute to a serene and prayerful mood.

If a quiet place is not available, or if you pray as you commute to and from work, remember that the God who loves you is present everywhere and hears your prayer no matter the setting.

I will bless the Lord at all times.

His praise will be ever on my lips.

Glory to the Father, and to the Son, and to the Holy Spirit,

As it was in the beginning, is now, and will be forever. Amen.

Psalm 91

God is my help and my protector.

One who dwells in the shelter of the Most High,

lives under the shadow of the Almighty.

Since you have made your dwelling

in the Most High, in the LORD your refuge,

evil shall not befall you,

and no plague will come close to your tent,

for he will command his angels

to guard you wherever you go:

they will carry you on their hands,

lest you strike your foot against a stone.

You will tread upon lions and vipers,

trample on lion cubs and dragons.

"Since you lovingly cling to me, I will rescue you;

I will bring you to safety since you have not ignored my name.

You will invoke me and I will answer you.

I myself will be with you when you are in distress:

I will draw you out and give you glory.
I will grant you the satisfaction of a long life
and let you enjoy my salvation."
Glory to the Father....

Psalm 103

May everyone praise God's holy name.

The LORD has his throne firmly set in heaven
and his royal sovereignty rules over all.
Bless the LORD, all you his angels,
powerful beings, fulfilling his will
by obeying the word he utters.
Bless the LORD, all you his hosts,
his servants, who carry out his wishes.
Bless the LORD, all you his creatures
in every place he rules.
My soul, bless the LORD!
Glory to the Father....

The Word of God   Tobit 12:15ff.

If we keep our priorities straight, the things of this world can lead us closer to God and help us enjoy true peace. Living in the presence of God gives real purpose to our lives.

I am Raphael, one of the seven holy angels who present the prayers of holy people and who stand before the glory of the Lord.

Do not be afraid; be at peace! Bless God always, for I did not come on my own account but because God willed it. Bless him forever. Bless and give thanks to God.

In the presence of the angels, I will sing your praises, Lord.

———— ✺ ————

From prayer one draws the strength needed to meet the challenges of daily life as a committed follower of Jesus Christ, and as such to be a living sign of the Lord's loving presence in the world.

Intercessions

L ord, I rejoice in the gift of a new day, coming into your presence to seek your grace and blessing:
Response: *I hope in you, Lord, I trust in your word.*

Inspire my thoughts, words and actions so that all I do today will serve your kingdom here on earth. **R.**

Remove from my heart all bitterness and pettiness, that I may bring happiness and encouragement to all whom I meet. **R.**

Help me to use my gifts and talents to generously serve the needs of others. **R.**

Give me understanding and patience that I may be an instrument of your love today. **R.**

Grant that all whom I love may spend this day in joy of spirit and peace of mind. **R.**

(Add your own general intentions and your particular intentions for this novena.)

Conclude your intercessions by praying to our Heavenly Father in the words Jesus taught us:

Our Father, who art in heaven, hallowed be thy name; thy kingdom come; thy will be done on earth as it is in heaven. Give us this day our daily bread, and forgive us our trespasses, as we forgive those who trespass against us, and lead us not into temptation, but deliver us from evil. Amen.

Closing Prayer

*L*ord, our God, let the splendor of your love light my way. As I begin this day in dedication to you, keep me true to your teaching and free from all sin. I ask this through Jesus Christ, your Son. Amen.

Let us praise the Lord
And give him thanks.

Novena to St. Raphael

O St. Raphael, bearer of holy joy and messenger of peace,

—*intercede for us before God's holy throne.*

You are one of the seven angels who enter and serve before the glory of the Lord,

—*present my prayer of praise and supplication at the throne of God.*

Prayer: *O God,* you brought joy of spirit and health in mind and body into the lives of Tobit, Sarah and Tobiah through your holy angel, Raphael. Grant, we beseech you, the grace we ask through the intercession of St. Raphael. Amen.

(Mention your petition and pray one Our Father, Hail Mary and Glory.)

Our Father, who art in heaven, hallowed be thy name; thy kingdom come; thy will be done on earth as it is in heaven. Give us this day our daily bread, and forgive us our trespasses, as we forgive those who trespass against us, and lead us not into temptation, but deliver us from evil. Amen.

Hail Mary, full of grace, the Lord is with you. Blessed are you among women, and blessed is the fruit of your womb, Jesus. Holy Mary, Mother of God, pray for us sinners, now and at the hour of our death. Amen.

Glory to the Father, and to the Son, and to the Holy Spirit, as it was in the beginning, is now, and will be forever. Amen.

Prayers for Various Needs

Prayer for Travelers

St. Raphael, Archangel, as you protected young Tobiah on his journey to a distant land, protect all those who travel today, especially *(name)*. Safeguard all fathers and mothers whose work requires them to travel; protect all children who travel to and from school, to be with a parent or visit a relative. Watch over those who journey to preach the Gospel. Guide those responsible for operating transport vehicles and inspire the owners of transportation systems to provide dependable and affordable means. Encourage those who maintain these systems to be trustworthy in providing safe and reliable means so that all who travel will reach their destinations in comfort and safety. Amen.

A Commuter's Prayer

St. Raphael, Archangel, you brought healing, joy and harmony to all those you met while you journeyed with young Tobiah. I, too, place myself under your protection as I commute today. Teach me how to be a bearer of God's healing peace as you were; let my words and actions reflect the kindness and compassion of Jesus. Be with me today and every day as I travel along the road of life. Amen.

A Driver's Prayer

Heavenly Father, grant me a steady hand and a watchful eye that I may safely reach my destination. Grant me self-control, a watchful eye and freedom from aggressive behavior. Protect those who travel with me today. For those whom I drive or meet, let me be thoughtful and courteous so that I can, in some small way, mirror the love Jesus has for each of us. Open the eyes of my heart that I may see beyond the road and skyscrapers to recognize the beauty that reflects the wonders of your creation.

St. Raphael, Archangel, be my guide and protector today. Kindly precede me and guard me. Amen.

Prayer Before Leaving for a Trip

*H*eavenly Father, we thank you for having created a great and wonderful world through which we can travel. We ask you to bless us as we are about to leave on our trip. In days past you sent your Archangel Raphael to accompany Tobiah on his journey; send him now to be with us as our guide and companion.

Deliver us from all harm and keep us safe in your love. Grant that we may rejoice in all that we see and all whom we meet. Free us from restlessness and disappointment due to delays or unpleasant weather. Give us patience to accept these with a spiritual vision, seeing in these events the mystery of your loving plan.

Let us awake each day to the beauty of creation that surrounds us and to a confident awareness of your sacred presence within. May your blessing be upon us to bring us home again in safety and in peace. Amen.

Prayer for Someone Leaving for a Trip

*H*eavenly Father, thank you for having created a great and wonderful world through which we can travel. I ask you to bless *(name)* who is leaving for *(place)*. In days past you sent your Archangel Raphael to accompany Tobiah on his journey; please send him now to be with *(name)* as her/his guide and companion.

Deliver her/him from all harm and keep her/him safe in your love. Grant that *(name)* may rejoice in all that she/he sees and all whom she/he meets. Free *(name)* from restlessness and disappointment due to delays or unpleasant weather. Give her/him patience to accept these with a spiritual vision, seeing in these events the mystery of your loving plan.

Let her/him awake each day to the beauty of creation that surrounds us and to a confident awareness of your sacred presence within. May your blessing be upon *(name)* to bring her/him home again in safety and in peace. Amen.

Prayer for Healing

Almighty and eternal God, healer of those who trust in you, through the intercession of St. Raphael, Archangel, hear my prayer for *(name)*. In your tender mercy, restore her/him to spiritual and/or bodily health that she/he may give you thanks, praise your name, and proclaim your wondrous love to all. I ask this through Christ your Son, our Lord. Amen.

Prayer for the Choice of a Spouse

St. Raphael, Archangel, sent by God to counsel young Tobiah in the choice of a good and virtuous spouse, guide me also in this important life-choice. With your help I want to meet the one who is "right for me," as a husband/wife. Through your inspiration I want my heart's choice to be the spouse the Lord would also choose for me, so that our life together will be one of mutual happiness and love. Amen.

Prayer for Newlyweds

$\mathcal{E}$ ternal and loving God, bless with your grace (*names*) who have sealed and strengthened their love through Christian marriage.

Grant that they may always rejoice in each other, in their mutual and lasting fidelity, and their undivided affection welling up from the fountain of your love. Grant that they may always remain faithful in body, mind and heart, in good times and in bad. Teach them to care for each other's needs, to communicate to one another their hopes and dreams, even sharing their fears and doubts. Enlighten them to reverence the mystery of their individuality, respect the gift of their equality, and recognize the uniqueness of their complementarity. Teach them compassion and forgiveness, that they may be instruments of your mercy and love to one another.

Together may they harvest spiritual riches by the practice of their faith, and ever be examples of faithfulness and love for the whole Christian family. Grant them many happy years together so that they may enjoy the gifts of a good life. And after they have served your kingdom here on earth, welcome them into your eternal kingdom of heaven. I ask all this through Christ, your Son. Amen. (*Adapted from the Rite of Marriage*)

Newlyweds' Prayer

St. Raphael not only guided Tobiah in finding his wife, Sarah, he also counseled them to pray together to ask God's blessings on their marriage.

Eternal and loving God, we thank you for sealing and strengthening our love through Christian marriage. Now we come before you to ask your grace-filled blessing.

Grant that we may always rejoice in each other, in our mutual and lasting fidelity, and our undivided affection welling up from the fountain of your love. Grant that we may always remain faithful in body, mind and heart, in good times and in bad. Teach us how to care for each other's needs, to communicate to one another our hopes and dreams, even sharing our fears and doubts. Enlighten us to reverence the mystery of our individuality, respect the gift of our equality, and recognize the uniqueness of our complementarity. Teach us to be compassionate and forgiving, that we may be instruments of your mercy and love to one another.

Together may we harvest spiritual riches by the practice of our faith, and ever be examples of faithfulness and love for the whole Christian family. Grant us many happy years together so that we may enjoy the gifts of a good life. And after we have served your kingdom here on earth, welcome us into your eternal kingdom of heaven. We ask all this through Christ, your Son. Amen. (*Adapted from the Rite of Marriage*)

Prayer of Praise and Thanksgiving

It is fitting for us to praise and thank God for the graces and privileges he has bestowed upon his angels and saints. Devotees of Saint Raphael may pray the following act of thanksgiving during their novena.

All-loving God, I praise, glorify and bless you for all the graces and privileges you have bestowed upon your messenger and servant, St. Raphael. By the merits of your angels grant me your grace, and through the intercession of your Archangel Raphael help me in all my needs. At the hour of my death be with me until that time when I can join the angels and saints in heaven to praise you forever and ever. Amen.

Evening Prayer

*A*s this day draws to a close we place ourselves in an attitude of thanksgiving. We take time to express our gratitude to a loving God for his abiding presence. We thank him for the gift of the day and all it brought with it. We thank him for all the things we were able to achieve throughout the day, and we entrust to him the concerns we have for tomorrow.

From the rising to the setting of the sun,
May the name of the Lord be praised.
Glory to the Father, and to the Son, and to the
    Holy Spirit,
As it was in the beginning, is now, and will be
    forever. Amen.

Take a few moments for a brief examination of conscience. Reflect on the ways God acted in your life today, how you responded to his invitations to think, speak and act in a more Christlike manner, and in what ways you would like to be a more faithful disciple tomorrow.

In your love and mercy, forgive me, Lord:

For the times I acted or spoke unkindly toward others.

Lord, have mercy.

For the times I failed to be generous and loving toward my spouse and children.

Christ, have mercy.

For the times I was untruthful or unforgiving.

Lord, have mercy.

For the times I raised my voice in anger, sarcasm or gossip.

Christ have mercy.

For the times…(any other petitions for pardon). (Or any other Act of Sorrow.)

Psalm 34

With the angels, I will sing your praises, O God.

I will bless the LORD at all times;
his praise is ever on my lips.
It is in the LORD that my soul shall boast.
The humble shall hear of it and rejoice.
Join me in celebrating the greatness of the LORD,
and let us extol his name together.
I sought the LORD and he answered me;

he delivered me from all my fears.
Those who gazed on him were radiant with joy
and their faces were not made to blush.
The afflicted ones cried out and the LORD heard,
and saved them from all their troubles.
The angel of the LORD is encamped
round about those who fear him, and delivers them.
Taste and see how good the LORD is.
Happy the person who takes refuge in him.
Glory to the Father....

The Word of God   Tobit 4:19

The advice which Tobiah received from his father invites us to welcome the Lord into the everyday circumstances of our lives. If we allow God to help us, our lives can be less complicated and more focused.

*I*n all circumstances bless the Lord and ask him to make your ways upright; and to make your plans and projects succeed because not every nation has true wisdom. It is the Lord who gives everything and he humbles those whom he wishes. My child, remember my advice and do not let it be erased from your heart.

Open my heart to the power of your word.

*In prayer we bring before the Lord our own needs
and the needs of those we love. We take time to consider
the needs of the world and intercede for those who do not
or cannot pray. We offer petitions for the improvement
of the human condition so that our world will be a better
place to live, and all people may contribute to building
up God's kingdom here on earth.*

Intercessions

*G*racious Lord, we thank you for the graces and
blessings you have given us. At the close of
this day we come before you to offer our needs and
the needs of all your people.

**Response: *Receive our prayer through the interces-
sion of St. Raphael.***

Bless all church leaders; may they be holy and
seek to be true witnesses to the gospel message of
love and compassion. **R.**

Bless all those who travel to preach the message
of God's love; may they be sustained in body and
spirit. **R.**

Bless world leaders; may they govern with integ-
rity and justice, safeguarding the rights of all human
persons, especially the weak and defenseless. **R.**

Bless all who are newly united in marriage; may the grace of the sacrament keep them faithful in body, mind and heart, in good times and in bad. **R.**

Bless husbands and wives; may they forever rejoice in each other and in their mutual and lasting fidelity. **R.**

Bless those who struggle with relationships in the home and in the workplace; may they find harmony and peace through your life-giving grace. **R.**

Bless all who travel or commute; may they be delivered from all harm and remain safe in your love. **R.**

Bless all who suffer in body, mind or spirit; may they experience the touch of the Divine Healer. **R.**

Bless all who have died; may they soon enjoy the peace and happiness of heaven. **R.**

(*Add any other spontaneous intentions and your particular intentions for this novena.*)

Conclude your intercessions by praying to our Heavenly Father in the words Jesus taught us:

Our Father, who art in heaven....

Closing Prayer

All-loving God, as evening falls and this day draws to a close, remain with us. Bring us safely through the night so that with the coming of the dawn we may give you praise and serve you more faithfully. We ask this through Jesus Christ, your Son. Amen.

Mary, Jesus' Mother and ours, is always ready to intercede for those who ask her help.

Remember, O most gracious Virgin Mary, that never was it known that anyone who fled to your protection, implored your help or sought your intercession, was left unaided. Inspired with this confidence, I fly to you, O Virgin of virgins, my Mother; to you I come; before you I kneel, sinful and sorrowful. O Mother of the Word Incarnate, despise not my petitions, but in your mercy hear and answer them. Amen.

May God's blessing remain with us forever. In the name of the Father, and of the Son, and of the Holy Spirit. Amen.

BOOKS & MEDIA

The Daughters of St. Paul operate book and media centers at
the following addresses. Visit, call or write the one nearest you
today, or find us on the World Wide Web, www.pauline.org

CALIFORNIA
3908 Sepulveda Blvd, Culver City,
  CA 90230   310-397-8676
2640 Broadway Street, Redwood City,
  CA 94063   650-369-4230
5945 Balboa Avenue, San Diego,
  CA 92111   858-565-9181

FLORIDA
145 S.W. 107th Avenue, Miami,
  FL 33174   305-559-6715

HAWAII
1143 Bishop Street, Honolulu,
  HI 96813   808-521-2731
Neighbor Islands call:
  866-521-2731

ILLINOIS
172 North Michigan Avenue, Chicago,
  IL 60601   312-346-4228

LOUISIANA
4403 Veterans Memorial Blvd,
  Metairie, LA 70006   504-887-7631

MASSACHUSETTS
Rte. 1, 885 Providence Hwy, Dedham,
  MA 02026   781-326-5385

MISSOURI
9804 Watson Road, St. Louis,
  MO 63126   314-965-3512

NEW JERSEY
561 U.S. Route 1, Wick Plaza,
  Edison, NJ 08817   732-572-1200

NEW YORK
150 East 52nd Street, New York,
  NY 10022   212-754-1110

OHIO
2105 Ontario Street, Cleveland,
  OH 44115   216-621-9427

PENNSYLVANIA
9171-A Roosevelt Blvd, Philadelphia,
  PA 19114   215-676-9494

SOUTH CAROLINA
243 King Street, Charleston,
  SC 29401   843-577-0175

TENNESSEE
4811 Poplar Avenue, Memphis,
  TN 38117   901-761-2987

TEXAS
114 Main Plaza, San Antonio,
  TX 78205   210-224-8101

VIRGINIA
1025 King Street, Alexandria,
  VA 22314   703-549-3806

CANADA
3022 Dufferin Street, Toronto,
  Ontario, Canada M6B 3T5
  416-781-9131

¡También somos su fuente para libros,
videos y música en español!